CHARM IS DECEITFUL AND BEAUTY IS PASSING,
BUT A WOMAN WHO FEARS THE LORD,
SHE SHALL BE PRAISED.

Proverbs 31:30 NKJV

Lesson 3
Titus 2:1-4

God's Beautiful Design for Women

But as for you, speak the things which are proper for sound doctrine: that the older men be sober, reverent, temperate, sound in faith, in love, in patience; the older women likewise, that they be reverent in behavior, not slanderers, not given to much wine, teachers of good things — that they admonish the young women to love their husbands, to love their children

This Week's Focus

The Titus 2 Woman

Perhaps there is nothing as beautiful in the Word of God as His plan for women as they age and mature. In Chapter 2 of Titus, God issues His mandate for women – older women are instructed to train the younger women in godly living, so that a legacy will be established for succeeding generations.

God wants each generation to know Him personally and have the joy of living an abundant life full of purpose and fruitfulness. He wants the world to know that living life His way works; because He loves us and wants our best. Not only that, He wants His daughters to walk in obedience so that His Word is not dishonored.

A Titus 2 woman is not meant to be an inspirational picture of virtuous women from long ago. Actually it is quite the opposite. God's Word presents the Titus Two woman as God's plan, God's desire, and God's marching orders for all women in Christ of any age in any era.

What does she look like today? The Titus 2 woman is saved by grace, and energized by the Spirit of God to live such an extraordinary life that the world, her husband, and her children all notice that she is different because she is in step with the Spirit and Word of God. As the Titus 2 woman ages, she becomes more beautiful and more fruitful. Her life is marked by her love for God and His Word. She finds her strength in His endless grace and is able to live each day in the Lord.

If married, she is a wife who loves her husband in such a profound way that he is deeply satisfied in her love; and if she is a mother, her children know they are deeply loved. Whether single or married, mother, wife, or alone; she is a woman that over the long haul radiates love, contentment, peace, and joy.

Age alone, however, does not qualify an older woman to leave a godly legacy. Titus outlines character qualities that define who this older woman is to be in order for her to train young women. The commission to train the younger generation of women is given to older, mature Christian women who have faithfully built into their own lives the message they are to impart to others.

This Week's Memory Verse

Charm is deceitful and beauty is passing, but a woman who fears the Lord, she shall be praised. Proverbs 31:30 NKJV

Where is the Titus 2 Woman?

Many women's ministries are struggling with keeping their mentoring ministries available to the body. It is not for a lack of young women mentees – there are not enough mentors to go around. Unfortunately older women often fall into a faulty mindset that "they have done their time" or they feel they have nothing to offer. Many feel they have nothing in common with younger women. Of course we know that this reasoning is not at all biblical.

1. Write Titus 2:3-5. How does this biblical mandate counter the above arguments about older women?

2. Age alone does not qualify an older woman to leave a godly legacy. Titus outlines character qualities that define who an older woman is to be in order for her to train young women. What are the five character qualities of the Titus 2 woman?

3. How old is old? Certainly the 20 something who loves God and His Word has something to offer someone younger. Give an example of opportunities for "younger women" to serve in Titus roles.

4. Have you believed the lie that you have nothing to offer a woman younger than yourself? Why or why not?

5. How does busyness hinder the progress of Titus 2 ministry?

6. How can a church hinder the progress of Titus 2 ministry?

The Beauty of Reverent Behavior

The Titus 2 woman who is reverent in her behavior sees life, all of life, from God's viewpoint and understands that even the mundane routines of life are important to God. Her lifestyle tells a watchful observer where her priorities are. If you were to watch her throughout her day, you would discover that she walks very closely to God. Her actions clearly flow from a heart that desires to live for God. Her life revolves around things that matter to Him.

How did she arrive at this place in her life? She has kept and continues to keep her relationship with God first. He is her first love and her first priority. God's Word is her source of truth and as she abides in relationship with Him, His power is continually available to her.

The woman who is reverent in her behavior consistently spends time studying God's Word, in order to stay in communion with the Father. She understands that the Word of God is the foundation for understanding God's character, His will, and what pleases Him. The reverent woman fears God, walking by faith in obedience to His Word. Her choices and decisions are godly, based on her respect and trust in God and His ways.

It is impossible to be a woman who is reverent in her behavior without the foundation of God's Word, and without a choice to obey God by faith. Over time, the woman who consistently responds in obedience to God's principles will become mature. A mature woman possesses a "God consciousness" that influences her daily regimen. She evaluates every thought, action, and encounter by the standard of the Bible.

Truth lights her path so that she can choose obedient behavior which is an outward expression of a heart that knows and communes with the Father.

Simply put, the woman who is reverent in her behavior is passionately in love with her Savior; her reverence, or "God-fearing" behavior, flows from a cultivated heart-life with the Father. She loves the truth of the Bible, not as an end in itself, but as a vehicle which leads her into intimate communication with her Father. She understands who God is, and goes heart-to-heart to keep the fine edge of her walk with God sharply honed.

1. Knowing God's Word is **key** to reverent behavior. Note the principle from each of the following verses that supports a woman in her desire to be a Titus 2 model.

    - Psalm 119:105

- Proverbs 9:10

- Romans 10:17

- 2 Corinthians 10:3-5

- 2 Timothy 2:15

- Hebrews 4:12

- Hebrews 11:6

- James 1:22

2. Do you see all of life from God's viewpoint? Why or why not?

3. How do you keep God and His Word as the first priority in your life?

4. In verse 3 of chapter 2, we often overlook the word **LIKEWISE** – which means *in the same manner*. So as the men were instructed in verse 2 to be: sober, reverent, temperate, sound in faith, in love, in patience; so we too should seek those character traits in our own life.

Patience is a fruit of the spirit we can all seek to possess more of. This quality can be described as cheerful endurance. How are you doing in the area of patience?

5. How can we develop patience in our life? Why is this character trait stressed throughout Scripture? What are the dangers of impatience?

6. Are you growing in love for others? How can you tell?

7. Look up the word "slanderer" in a Bible dictionary. Gossip is said to be a close cousin to slander. How so? Why is it important that women not be involved in slander?

8. What are some practical ways to teach a young woman how to love her husband?

9. What are some practical ways to teach a young woman how to parent her children?

10. Who is a Christian woman that you admire? Why do you esteem her?

This Week's Application

1. Have you benefited from a Titus 2 relationship in your life? If so, how? If not, how would a Titus 2 relationship help you in your life right now?

2. If you are a seasoned believer with a love for God and His Word – are you involved in a Titus 2 relationship? If so describe that relationship and what you enjoy about it. If not, what do you feel has kept you from reaching out to a younger woman?

3. What are some creative ways to be a Titus 2 woman to the younger women around you?

4. How can taking your place as a Titus 2 woman help you to be a godly woman in the culture you live in today? How can it impact the life of others?

This Week's Challenge

Pray and ask God to lead you to a young woman in need of discipleship. Be willing to make a short-term time commitment (three to six months). Provide the space in your life to meet with her on a regular basis, preferably weekly, for one to two hours. Be creative. Come up with a plan that will work for you and benefit the young woman. Here are a few ideas to consider:

- Go through a book together – "Becoming God's True Woman" by Nancy Leigh De Moss is a good choice.
- Read and journal through one of the gospels, then meet to exchange thoughts and share what each of you learned.
- Offer to show her what you've learned about meal planning, grocery shopping, cleaning, time management, etc.

Note: If you are a young woman in need of an older woman to come alongside you – pray and ask God who you should approach.

This Week's Digging Deeper

It is important that we view ourselves as women, **"biblically"**. Take time this week to join Titus 2:3-5 with Proverbs 31:10-31 and 1 Peter 3:1-6.

- What do you discover?

- How does "biblical womanhood" stand in direct opposition to "worldly womanhood"?

- Have you been tempted to fall into the world's idea of "womanhood"? Why or why not?

AS A RING OF GOLD IN A SWINE'S SNOUT,
SO IS A LOVELY WOMAN WHO LACKS DISCRETION.

Proverbs 11:22 NKJV

Lesson 4
Titus 2:5

Discretion: A Lost Virtue

To be discreet, chaste, homemakers, good, obedient to their own husbands, that the word of God may not be blasphemed.

This Week's Focus

Imagine a pig with a gold ring through its nose. Not many people would pierce a pig for decoration, but the writer of the Proverb was trying to make a point. The gold ring is not becoming to the pig. The grossness of the filthy pig far outweighs the beauty of the jewelry.

Now imagine a beautiful woman who has no self-control. The grossness of her conduct far outweighs her beauty. That is the essence of the Proverb: "As a ring of gold in a swine's snout, so is a lovely woman who lacks discretion." (Proverbs 11:22, NKJV) To God, this is a serious issue. To compare the character of an Israelite woman to a pig was unheard of, an extreme insult. But it communicated an important lesson that women of today can learn from.

Discretion has many facets, all are equally important. A woman who is discreet in outward character is able to carry herself without fear. She conducts herself with wisdom, not trying to draw attention to herself. She knows how to avoid embarrassment. A woman with inward discretion is cautious in making her decisions. She is careful to discern all the facts, taking heed to wise counsel before moving ahead. In short, a discreet woman uses **self-control** *in all areas of her life.*

Indiscreet women feel the need to be seen. They are loud, aggressive, arrogant, impulsive, and the like. They draw attention to themselves by trying to appear to have it all together. They are thoughtless in their speech, talking incessantly about whatever comes to mind. They operate based on whatever they feel or think at the moment. They are oblivious to how their actions affect other people. Their insecurity drives them to flaunt themselves, both in behavior and appearance. They dress in such a way to draw attention to themselves, with tinkling jewelry, gaudy makeup, tight fitting clothes, and so on.

In contrast, God has called Christian women to stand out from the women of the world. They are to be an example of how God created a woman to be. A Christian woman with discretion does not need to be the center of attention. Instead, she finds her security in her relationship with Jesus Christ. She is not quick to flaunt what she knows, or what she looks like. She is not impulsive, or loud. She does not talk about everything that comes to mind. Though she may have an outgoing personality, she is happy to be silent and hidden. Rather than a pig with a ring of gold through its snout, she is a like a rare gem that is quarried from deep within the earth, hidden for a time until discovered by those who recognize her true beauty and value.

This Week's Memory Verse

As a ring of gold in a swine's snout, so is a lovely woman who lacks discretion. Proverbs 11:22 NKJV

This Week's Time in the Word

1. How is the virtue of **"discretion"** disappearing from our culture today?

2. How would you help a young woman who had a problem with **"discretion"**?

3. What Scriptures would you lead her to effectively "teach" her in the area of discretion?

4. Let's take a good look at ourselves. What are some ways we can be "indiscreet"?

It is always a good exercise towards godliness in our lives to take a spiritual assessment of our lives and closely examine our hearts. Nancy Leigh De Moss offers a valuable inventory we can use to measure our becoming virtuous women. Pray and ask the Holy Spirit to reveal any areas in your mind, heart and life that may be hindering you from operating in the fullness of His Spirit. Take your time this week to consider these questions. Answer honestly and allow the Lord to work so that you may grow in the area of discretion and help other women to do the same.

Write Proverbs 14:1

For the Married Woman

1. Am I building up my house or tearing it down?

2. Am I investing in my marriage? Am I nurturing the heart of my marriage?

3. Do I frequently express admiration and gratitude to my husband?

4. Am I reserving the best of my physical and emotional energy for my family?

5. Am I creating an atmosphere (through words, actions, and attitudes) that makes my husband desire to be at home?

6. Am I content to be "at home"? Am I finding my "fulfillment" through reverencing and serving my husband and family?

7. Do I reserve intimate communication, looks, words, and touch for my husband? Am I giving of my emotions, attention, affection to a man other than my husband?

8. Am I meeting my husband's sexual needs?

9. Am I trustworthy? Is there any behavior or relationship I am involved in that I am keeping from my husband? Have I been totally honest with my husband?

10. Does my husband have the freedom to be totally honest with me?

11. Am I looking to a man other than my husband (pastor, counselor, colleague) to be a primary source of counsel or to fill an emotional vacuum in my life?

12. Do I have a more intimate relationship—physically, emotionally, or spiritually—with any man than I do with my husband?

For the Married and Single Woman

13. Am I fueling sensual thoughts and desires through books, magazines, TV programs, music, or movies that are not morally pure?

14. Have I become a "refuge" for a man who may be struggling in his marriage?

15. Does my demeanor tend to be "loud and defiant," or do I communicate a meek, quiet, and submissive spirit?

16. Am I a "wall" or a "door" (Song of Songs 8:12)? Am I a "loose" woman? Do I communicate to the men around me that I am "available"? Does my demeanor invite them to "partake" of intimate parts of my body, soul, or spirit? Do I engage in flirtatious speech, looks, or behavior?

17. Is there anything about my speech, actions, dress, or attitudes that could defraud the men around me?

18. Am I discreet and restrained in the way I talk with men at work? Is my conversation ever loose, crude, or unbecoming for a woman of God? Am I expressing admiration for a man that should more appropriately come from his wife?

19. Does my dress help men to keep their thoughts pure and Christ-centered? Is my dress feminine and modest?

20. Have I erected (and am I maintaining) adequate "hedges" in my relationships with men? What are those hedges?

21. Am I currently in a situation that is (or could become) compromising? Am I in a situation that could appear to others to be compromising?

22. Would men and women who know me, say that I am a woman of moral virtue and purity?

23. Have I purposed in my heart to be morally pure? Am I making myself accountable to another godly woman for my walk with God and others?

Write Proverbs 31:30. How does this verse build upon the truths that you are learning today?

This Week's Application

1. What can you apply to your life today that you learned in this week's study?

2. How will you follow through?

3. A woman of "discretion" is meant to be a "stand out" – a "stand out" for Christ. Are you being effective in standing out for Christ in your home, in your neighborhood, in your workplace, in the church, in ministry? Why or Why not?

4. How can the virtue of "discretion" help you to live as a godly woman in today's culture?

This Week's Challenge

How can you quickly remedy an area in your life where you noticed you have been "indiscreet"? Pray and ask God to empower to you to walk in a greater degree of discretion. If you need accountability in areas where you are being tempted, give a sister in Christ a call and ask her to help you.

This Week's Digging Deeper

- Define the word, "**blasphemy**".

- How is the Word of God blasphemed by our disobedience?

- How can this be a serious issue as we seek to teach others?

- Give some examples of blaspheming the Word of God and provide some ways in your life to safeguard against **"blasphemy"** of the Word of God. Use Scripture to support your answer.

LET NO ONE DESPISE YOUR YOUTH,
BUT BE AN EXAMPLE TO THE BELIEVERS IN WORD,
IN CONDUCT, IN LOVE, IN SPIRIT, IN FAITH, IN PURITY.

1 Timothy 4:12 NKJV

Lesson 5
Titus 2:6-10

A Pattern of Good Works

Likewise, exhort the young men to be sober-minded, in all things showing yourself to be a pattern of good works; in doctrine showing integrity, reverence, incorruptibility, sound speech that cannot be condemned, that one who is an opponent may be ashamed, having nothing evil to say of you. Exhort bondservants to be obedient to their own masters, to be well pleasing in all things, not answering back, not pilfering, but showing all good fidelity, that they may adorn the doctrine of God our Savior in all things. Titus 2:6-10

This Week's Focus

Titus, being a young man himself, was to be an example of the sensible, self-controlled believer. The young men he taught needed a model for Christian living, and this young pastor must be "showing [himself] to be a pattern of good works."

Timothy, the contemporary of Titus, was also a young pastor ministering in Ephesus. To him Paul said, "Let no one despise your youth, but be an example to the believers in word, in conduct, in love, in spirit, in faith, in purity". That listing of areas in which Timothy was to be an example to other Christians is an expansion of what is referred to here in Titus 2:7 as "all things."

The need for Titus to be a pattern" (Greek - tupos; "a blow") is better understood from the word itself which translates a term originally describing the impression made on a surface by a stamp or a seal. Whenever the stamp or seal received the strike or "the blow" of the hammer, it left a pattern of the stamp or seal on that surface. The emphasis is not on the stamp but on the force used to push it into the material being stamped. The force -- not the stamp -- left a lasting impression.

In the hands of God, Titus could make a powerful impression in the lives of those to whom he ministered. In turn, they would have the same influence on others, but it was God at work in them all. The Holy Spirit who, through self-control, made Titus a living picture of sensibility and godliness would impress that same image of holy living on the hearts of other Christians. That would occur as they watched this young man put God's word into practice. This week we will learn how to be "patterns of good works" as we seek to live as godly women in today's culture.

This Week's Memory Verse

Let no one despise your youth, but be an example to the believers in word, in conduct, in love, in spirit, in faith, in purity. 1 Timothy 4:12 NKJV

This Week's Time in the Word

1. It has been said **"Example must follow advice"**. How does this apply to what we are studying?

2. Paul wanted Titus to leave a mark on those God had given him to influence, and he wanted to strongly emphasize his obligation to be a stamp in the hands of the Lord as it were -- a model of what God can do through one who is sensible and self-controlled. The idea of pattern is not so much the stamp or the die but the hammer or pressure exerted to create the deepest expression "a figure formed by a blow or impression".

    What do you think this illustration was meant to teach Titus and us today?

3. Jeremiah 18:1-6 provides more insight.

4. How do you respond to situations when you are "under pressure"? Does your life during these times exhibit a pattern of good works? Why or why not?

5. Paul was specific in the areas he called Titus to be a good model. We discover those areas in verses 7-9. Make a list of those areas where Titus was to be a pattern of good works.

6. One of those areas where we are to be a pattern of good works is "sound speech"; in other words, healthy and wholesome speech.

    - What are some ways our speech can be used for evil? Use Scripture to support your answer.

7. What are some ways our speech can be used for good? Use Scripture to support your answer.

8. When is it hardest for you to control your tongue? What Scripture could you memorize to call upon when you are tempted to use your speech in the wrong way?

9. Why is it important that people have nothing evil to say of us? Build upon your answer by noting the following Scriptures:

- Matthew 5:13-16

- 2 Corinthians 3:2-3

- 2 Corinthians 5:20

10. How does 1 Peter 3:15-16 support what you have been studying?

11. Look up 2 or 3 other translations of Titus 2:10. What does it mean to **"adorn the doctrine of God"?**

- The idea here is that we are to "show the beauty of the teaching of God". We have the privilege as believers to reflect the beauty and value of God's Word by the way we live our lives.

This Week's Application

1. Though we are not slaves, we all have someone in authority over us that we are to submit to. Ephesians 6:5-7 and Colossians 3:23-24 help us to practically walk in today's passage. How should these verses impact our every day life as it relates to those who are in authority?

2. Joseph is a solid biblical example who adorned the doctrine of God even in difficult and unfair circumstances. What do you learn about Joseph from the following passages? How can you apply his example to your life?

    - Genesis 39:1-9

    - Genesis 50:15-21

3. What is a proper response for a believer as it relates to those in governmental authority? Use Scripture to support your answer.

4. In what areas of your life do you struggle with authority and why?

5. **Fidelity** is an important word especially as it relates to God. Define the meaning of the word **"fidelity"** and explain what Paul is saying when he asks us to "show all good fidelity".

6. How can living to be "a pattern of good works" help us to live as godly women in today's culture?

This Week's Challenge

Read Romans 12:9 – 13:7. Write down how you further learn how to adorn the doctrine of God in everyday life. Note the areas of your life where your attitudes and actions are less than Christ-like and ask for more of God's Spirit in your life.

This Week's Digging Deeper

Charles Finney was a leader in the Second Great Awakening. He has been called *The Father of Modern Revivalism*. Take time to read through his thoughts on adorning the gospel and highlight the statements that stand out to you. Journal your thoughts and seek the Lord in prayer as you desire to be one who adorns the gospel.

On Adorning the Gospel

To adorn it is to honor it, and make it honorable before all. It implies that we commend it by being ourselves an illustration of its meaning, and by evincing to all its spirit and efficacy. We are to prove the excellence of the doctrine by showing, in our own case, what it can do in the hands of the Holy Spirit to reform the world. The doctrine is good or otherwise, according to its practical results. If it accomplishes what it aims to, it is beyond expression valuable and glorious. That it can and does, is just the thing which God leaves for his people to prove by their lives. Hence, they must live so as to hold forth the excellence, beauty and power, of the gospel.

What are the particular reasons for our thus adorning the gospel?

Unless we adorn and honor the gospel, it will dishonor us. Paul said--"I magnify my office." He honored the office of an apostle and it honored him. But if he had neglected and disparaged the office, it would have visited disgrace on him. So if we do not magnify our office, all will despise us--the devil and all the universe will count us too mean to be cared for. To have such responsibilities and then to heed them not; to be pressed with such motives, and yet have no sensibility to their pressure and force--this would show that our character has no worthy elements in it, and ought to subject us to dishonor. If you do not adorn the gospel, there must be a reason; and what is it? This--that you are playing the hypocrite!

Again, if we do not adorn the gospel, it will more deeply ruin us. The gospel, instead of blessing us, will only work for us a deeper damnation. There is no avoiding such a result from such a life.

It will greatly grieve the Savior. If we profess the gospel and yet do not adorn it, we do the worst thing we can do to injure his cause and wound his feelings. Accordingly, we find that he expresses the utmost displeasure and disgust towards those who profess to love and honor him, yet do not. To one of the seven churches of Asia, he said--"I know thy works that thou art neither cold nor hot; I would thou wert cold or hot. So then, because thou art lukewarm and neither cold nor hot, I will spew thee out of my mouth!" No such language can be found elsewhere in the Bible;--from which we may infer that the Savior hates no other form of sin more intensely and with more utter loathing.

Again, if we do not adorn the gospel, we shall greatly hinder and retard its success. We shall stumble others who would enter the narrow way. Our life scandalizes the gospel which it should, but does not, adorn. He who, professing the gospel, does not adorn it, gives his highest influence against it. He throws against it the whole weight of his example.

If you reply to this that it is better to profess religion and be a somewhat decent backslider, than to come out in open opposition, this is not true. No argument which an opposer can use against the gospel will have the weight that a protesting life will have. He who professes love but lives hatred; whose lips honor Christ, but whose life protests against him, is Christ's worst enemy. The gospel does not suffer from any other foes as from him.

On the other hand, if we do adorn the gospel, it will surely adorn us. Let any one really adorn the gospel, it shall be to him a mantle of glory. If men witness in him the spirit of Christ, they will admire that spirit and honor him who exhibits it. Besides this, it will win others to love the Savior. If we illustrate it in our lives, it will carry conviction and persuasion too. It is true that in many things, the motives of Christians are liable to be misjudged. Sometimes, when they do right, false motives are imputed to them. Yet, though this be true, there will be many things which the world will be obliged to confess, and this reluctant testimony will be the more to their real honor. Wicked men cannot gainsay their living testimony to the power of the gospel on their own hearts, as manifest in their lives. A holy life will command the attention of the world, and they will inquire what this doctrine may be. They are forced to exclaim--How beautiful their lives are! and how sweet their temper! Who is this Savior whom they profess to follow, and to whose influence they attribute their peculiar spirit and life? If this doctrine begets such a spirit and such a life, we ought to know it and ought to have it!

So it will always be. If this doctrine is really adorned, it will be sure to create inquiry. It must arrest attention. There are probably few men of the least observation who have not known certain persons whose lives have arrested their attention. A man can hardly live anywhere without coming in contact with someone of whom he is constrained to ask--What is it that enables him to live so? What spirit is this? When they see its striking and beautiful manifestations, they are constrained to inquire thus for its causes, and are anxious to learn what they may be.

Journal your thoughts

FOR BY GRACE YOU HAVE BEEN SAVED
THROUGH FAITH, AND THAT NOT OF YOURSELVES;
IT IS THE GIFT OF GOD,

Ephesians 2:8 NKJV

Lesson 6
Titus 2:11-15

Trained by Grace

For the grace of God that brings salvation has appeared to all men, teaching us that, denying ungodliness and worldly lusts, we should live soberly, righteously, and godly in the present age, looking for the blessed hope and glorious appearing of our great God and Savior Jesus Christ, who gave Himself for us, that He might redeem us from every lawless deed and purify for Himself His own special people, zealous for good works. Speak these things, exhort, and rebuke with all authority. Let no one despise you.

This Week's Focus

I'm sure you've noticed that when tragedy strikes in our nation, it is common for a performer to sing the hymn, "Amazing Grace." Certainly in a time of crisis even the world recognizes the need for divine compassion. But the grace of God John Newton wrote about in his famous hymn is not what people imagine it to be. The grace unfolded in our text is the transforming power of God that delivers us from sin and makes us new women in Christ.

The Biblical teaching of the Gospel of grace transforms people's lives. It powerfully leads away from sin and self-centeredness to godliness. It never fails to do so in a genuinely redeemed person. By the death of Christ, grace consecrates us to God for a life of good works. Certainly without God's grace, we could have no chance of living as godly women in today's culture.

The **Scofield Study Bible** aptly describes Titus 2:11-15 as one of the most concise summations in the entire New Testament of the relation of Gospel truth to life. May we allow ourselves this week to be trained by grace for an understanding of grace is at the heart of a victorious life in Jesus Christ.

This Week's Memory Verse

For by grace you have been saved through faith, and that not of yourselves; it is the gift of God,
Ephesians 2:8 NKJV

This Week's Time in the Word

GOD'S GRACE SAVES US

For the grace of God that brings salvation has appeared to all men. Titus 2:11

1. Grace rescues us from the greatest possible destruction – God's wrath upon sin. Grace communicates the heart of God, His compassion and kindness toward us. Grace meets us in our failure and sinful state and extends divine mercy toward us.

    Write your own definition of grace.

    When did God's grace first reach out to you?

2. Read Ephesians 1:7 and list a few of the reasons we are rich in God's grace.

3. Does the way you are living your life reflect your gratitude for God's grace – His redemption and forgiveness? Why or why not?

4. How can we best thank God for His amazing grace? (Romans 12:1-2)

GRACE TEACHES US HOW TO LIVE

Teaching us that, denying ungodliness and worldly lusts, we should live soberly, righteously, and godly in the present age   Titus 2:12

Grace comes bringing salvation and cannot fail to deliver those who believe its message.

Some of Paul's readers in Crete were still living a self-directed life. They were treating grace as if it were a license to pursue self-centered goals. Verse 12 teaches us that grace is not merely a "ticket" to heaven; **grace not only saves, but also teaches us how to live**.

Grace is a lifestyle that dramatically changes our entire orientation. It teaches us that friendship with the world is completely inconsistent for the true believer. If you are a genuine partaker of God's grace, then you will be motivated to live a godly and upright life not because of anything you have done or can do but because of what Christ has done for you!

Grace commands us, grace challenges us, grace calls us, grace cajoles us, grace caresses us into a life of worship and godliness, in which our only thought, our only objective, in all of our actions, should be to bring joy and glory to the One who has showered this grace upon us.

1. What do you learn about grace in Romans 6:1-4?

2. Many take grace to mean that people can live however they want --- how is this a serious misunderstanding of grace?

3. Read James 4:1-10 and record everything you learn about grace. What is the key to continually receiving the grace of God to help you to live a godly life?

4. Practically, how do we learn to live a godly life? Use Scripture to support your answer.

5. When you experience God's unmerited favor in Jesus Christ, it motivates you to want to please Him in everything that you do. Do you desire to please God in everything you do? Why or why not?

6. Titus 2 goes off like an alarm clock in the conscience; it wakes our slumbering consciences to the truth of what it means to be a partaker of God's grace. No one sleeps her way to heaven. Those bound for heaven are diligent students of grace, their teacher – they are "awake" in class learning the lessons taught by grace.

7. How are you growing in the grace of God?

GRACE WAITS AND LOOKS AHEAD

Looking for the blessed hope and glorious appearing of our great God and Savior Jesus Christ   Titus 2:13

We've seen that God's grace has appeared to helpless sinners, and that God's grace instructs believers in the art of living. But grace not only instructs our minds, but also our hearts in hope (how needed this is in a world that often lives on the edge of despair).

1. By the power of grace, what are we told in verse 13 that the Christian is waiting for?

2. Do you agree with the following statement? ***To the degree that a person is enamored with the world*** (and consequently lives in the flesh*) **she is ignorant of the importance of the promise of eternal life.*** Why or why not? Use Scripture to support your answer.

In today's culture women live pleasure-demanding lives. **But the Christian woman waits.** She is enabled by grace to spurn the pleasures of sin in order to follow Christ and gain eternal pleasure in the world to come. She looks beyond this life to the Blessed Hope.

3. We are awaiting the appearing of God's glory! The hope of glory is a powerful antidote to worldly living! Look up the following Scriptures and record what you learn about the hope of glory!

    - 2 Corinthians 3:18

    - Colossians 1:27

    - 1 Peter 1:6-8

    - 1 John 3:2-3

Once the anticipation of glory gets into your heart you will never be the same person. This is because grace is *educating* your hopes and making you *content to say no to sin, and follow Christ*.

GRACE PURIFIES

Who gave Himself for us, that He might redeem us from every lawless deed and purify for Himself His own special people, zealous for good works. Titus 2:14

1. In verse 14 we learn the purpose of Christ's work of redemption. What is it?

2. Paul wrote to a Mediterranean world that was very familiar with the concept of slaves obtaining freedom by means of the payment of a redemption price. The price of your freedom from the sphere and dominion of sin was the death of the Son of God. That means that those who know Christ as Savior will have transformed lives. The redeemed will not remain "in the jail" of sin's bondage.

   Imagine someone paying bail for your release from prison yet you remain in your cell. Freedom is yours but you remain imprisoned. Christ gave Himself for you. He has redeemed your life. Are you living free or in bondage to sin? Why or Why not?

Notice the purpose of Christ's work of redemption – it is that believers might be a people for God's own possession with a zest for good deeds. The purpose behind God's grace is to rescue us from wickedness and make us a people marked out by the fact that we are eagerly pursuing good in our lives.

3. How are you eagerly pursuing good in your life?

This Week's Application

1. You have worked hard this week! Take some time to write down everything you learned about grace and how you might apply it to your life.

2. One way we can tell if grace is having its work accomplished in our lives is by measuring how grace filled we are towards others. How do you show grace to the people God has placed in your life?

3. How does being trained by grace help you to live as a godly woman in today's culture?

This Week's Challenge

Read 2 Corinthians 12:1-10 and ask God to show you how His grace is sufficient for you. Write down what you learn and if you have a similar "thorn" like Paul's share how God's grace is helping you live with it.

This Week's Digging Deeper

Read the book of Galatians for a further study on grace. Jot down verses where Paul is teaching on grace and also note how easily we can run back to the law. Compare what you learned this week in Titus to what you discover in Galatians.

BUT SOMEONE WILL SAY,
"YOU HAVE FAITH, AND I HAVE WORKS."
SHOW ME YOUR FAITH WITHOUT YOUR WORKS,
AND I WILL SHOW YOU MY FAITH BY MY WORKS.

James 2:18 NKJV

Lesson 7
Titus 3:1-15

A Woman and Sound Doctrine

Remind them to be subject to rulers and authorities, to obey, to be ready for every good work, to speak evil of no one, to be peaceable, gentle, showing all humility to all men. For we ourselves were also once foolish, disobedient, deceived, serving various lusts and pleasures, living in malice and envy, hateful and hating one another. But when the kindness and the love of God our Savior toward man appeared, not by works of righteousness which we have done, but according to His mercy He saved us, through the washing of regeneration and renewing of the Holy Spirit, whom He poured out on us abundantly through Jesus Christ our Savior, that having been justified by His grace we should become heirs according to the hope of eternal life. This is a faithful saying, and these things I want you to affirm constantly, that those who have believed in God should be careful to maintain good works. These things are good and profitable to men. But avoid foolish disputes, genealogies, contentions, and strivings about the law; for they are unprofitable and useless. Reject a divisive man after the first and second admonition, knowing that such a person is warped and sinning, being self-condemned. When I send Artemas to you, or Tychicus, be diligent to come to me at Nicopolis, for I have decided to spend the winter there. Send Zenas the lawyer and Apollos on their journey with haste, that they may lack nothing. And let our people also learn to maintain good works, to meet urgent needs, that they may not be unfruitful. All who are with me greet you. Greet those who love us in the faith. Grace be with you all. Amen. Titus 3:1-15

This Week's Focus

This week we will study the foundation of what it is that we believe. We need to be continually reminded and think about what God has done for us so that our lives will be both useful and fruitful. Paul told Titus that he wanted believers to be affirmed constantly in these doctrinal truths and that when these foundational truths are understood, embraced and believed, good works would continually flow from their life – eternal fruit for the Kingdom.

This Week's Memory Verse

But someone will say, "You have faith, and I have works." Show me your faith without your works, and I will show you my faith by my works.
James 2:18 NKJV

SOUND DOCTRINE

1. Why is it so important that a woman knows what she believes?

SALVATION

> Salvation is a gift of God,
> Not something earned or won;
> He freely gives eternal life
> To all who trust His Son. —Sper

**We are saved by God's mercy, not by our merit—
by Christ's dying, not by our doing.**

2. What is Paul desiring us to know in Titus 3:8, 1Timothy 1:15 and 2 Timothy 2:11?

3. Aren't you thankful that God has acted on your behalf and saved you out of your foolishness? The appearance of the kindness and the love of God refer to Jesus. How does the love and kindness of God motivate us to a life of good works?

4. Compare Titus 3:4-7 and Ephesians 2:4-10. What do you learn about salvation?

THE HOLY SPIRIT AND ETERNAL LIFE

5. What do we discover about salvation and the Holy Spirit from John 3:1-8 and 1 Peter 1:3?

6. We are heirs according to the hope of eternal life. How does Ephesians 1:13-14 support this truth?

JUSTIFICATION

7. Those Titus mentions in verse 3 are justified in God's sight when they are saved, and it is all by God's grace. What does "justified" mean?

OUR MOTIVATION

8. What does 2 Corinthians 5:14-21 tell us?

9. Christ's love compels us so that we should no longer live for ourselves but for God. In what ways are you living for God?

10. Read James 3:13-18. How does this passage support how Titus is exhorting us to live?

This Week's Application

1. How should the doctrinal statements made in Titus 3 influence the behavior that Paul is asking Titus to exhort believers to?

2. We are to be peacemakers, ministers of reconciliation, and ambassadors for Christ.

    - **How are you doing in your relationships with believers?**

    - **With those in authority over you?**

    - **With unbelievers?**

3. Are you growing in the character traits of humility and gentleness that Paul exhorts us to? Why or why not?

4. How would growing in grace help your relationships with others?

5. What are some practical ways we can grow in grace?

6. How does grace enable us to maintain good works and stay aware of pressing needs?

7. How can sound doctrine and good works help you to be a godly woman in today's culture?

8. What are three of the most valuable truths you have gleaned from the Book of Titus? How will you practically work those truths into your life?

This Week's Challenge

Read through the Book of Titus again and write down everything you learn about the doctrine of the Trinity.

This Week's Digging Deeper

Paul's letters to Timothy have much in common and provide a deeper understanding of the Book of Titus. Read 1 and 2 Timothy taking note of the similarities to Titus. Also note key verses which highlight the truths you have learned in Titus.

ABOUT THE AUTHOR

Margy Hill's passion and calling for women's ministry led her to start the Women's Ministry Connection where she encourages and exhorts women leaders in ministry. God has given her the opportunity to speak into the lives of women of all ages and church backgrounds.

She loves to teach and share her passion for the Word of God to stir women to a deeper and more abundant relationship with Jesus and to encourage and equip them to walk in the fullness of their callings.

Her gift for writing has led her to write several Bible studies to help women develop a desire to dig deeper into the Word of God. With challenging questions and everyday application, her studies have been widely used throughout churches in the United States.

Margy speaks and teaches for women's conferences, retreats and seminars and is also known for her "Hope for the Hurting Heart" training seminars to help equip women to counsel confidently from the Word of God.

For more information, visit her website at www.wmconnection.org.

Printed in Great Britain
by Amazon.co.uk, Ltd.,
Marston Gate.